DRONES
EYES IN THE SKIES

ENTERTAINMENT DRONES

DANIEL R. FAUST

PowerKiDS
press

New York

Published in 2016 by The Rosen Publishing Group, Inc.
29 East 21st Street, New York, NY 10010

First Edition

Editor: Sarah Machajewski
Book Design: Reann Nye

Library of Congress Cataloging-in-Publication Data

Faust, Daniel R., author.
 Entertainment drones / Daniel R. Faust.
    pages cm. — (Drones : eyes in the skies)
 Includes bibliographical references and index.
 ISBN 978-1-5081-4493-9 (pbk.)
 ISBN 978-1-5081-4494-6 (6 pack)
 ISBN 978-1-5081-4495-3 (library binding)
 1. Drone aircraft—Juvenile literature. 2. Helicopters—Models—Radio control—Juvenile literature. 3. Amusements—Juvenile literature. I. Title.
 TL547.F3753 2016
 629.133—dc23
                                      2015029592

Manufactured in the United States of America

CPSIA Compliance Information: Batch #BW16PK: For Further Information contact Rosen Publishing, New York, New York at 1-800-237-9932

CONTENTS

WHAT IS A DRONE?

It seems like drones are everywhere. Every day, there's another story about them in the news. Do you know what a drone is? A drone is an unmanned aerial **vehicle**, or UAV. Drones are different from other aircraft because they don't carry a human pilot. A drone is either controlled by an onboard computer or flown from a remote location by a human pilot, who's sometimes called an operator.

The earliest drones were used by the military and **intelligence** agencies, such as the CIA. Drones can be flown over enemy territory to gather knowledge about possible threats without putting human pilots in danger. Some military drones are even equipped with weapons, such as missiles and bombs. Today, drones have many nonmilitary uses. Many industries, including the entertainment industry, are now exploring how they can use drones.

THAT'S SHOW BIZ!

The entertainment industry includes movies, television, radio, music, theater, and comedy.

When most people hear the word "drone," they probably think of the kind used by the military, like the MQ-1 Predator shown here.

DRONE BASICS

No matter what kind they are, all drones operate under the same basic principles. They need to create enough thrust, or forward motion, and lift to get off the ground and into the air. Some military drones have jet engines, but most drones available to the public are **rotorcraft**. Drones have simple **sensors** that keep them stable and help them avoid crashing into things.

Drones were designed to be flown remotely. Most drones are controlled by a simple radio transmitter, such as the kind used for radio-controlled cars and airplanes. The military and law enforcement agencies use drones that are controlled by large consoles, which are much like aircraft cockpits. Regular people can fly drones using a smartphone, tablet, or computer!

FLIGHT CONTROLLER

WHAT'S UNDER THE HOOD?

Even if a drone is flown remotely, it has a flight controller, which is also known as autopilot. Paired with a GPS, the flight controller can be programmed to fly the drone without a human operator.

Drones don't carry human pilots. Instead, they fly on their own, or they're controlled remotely by radio transmitters, such as the one pictured here. This model can also stream video through a smartphone.

A DRONE OF MANY USES

The first drones were designed by the military with very specific uses in mind. Military drones have video equipment and sensors that allow them to operate at night and during poor weather conditions. Intelligence agencies and law enforcement agencies use drones to survey large areas from above, patrol U.S. borders, and search for people on the run.

Though they're not as advanced as the drones used by the military, commercial, **civilian**, and entertainment drones have just as many uses. Because most drones can carry cameras, they've become popular tools for aerial filming and photography. This is helpful in the entertainment industry, where drones are used to film concerts and crowds.

Drones are now used to film or take pictures of extreme activities, including cool bike tricks!

9

CARRYING CAMERAS

Most of the drones available to people and businesses are based on a lightweight **quadcopter** design. The four rotors of these small drones are only powerful enough to carry small **payloads**. Cameras can be a fun addition to drones. Luckily, many digital cameras are light enough for a drone to carry.

Not only do cameras record overhead footage, they can also be programmed to stream live video of what the drone "sees" to a laptop, smartphone, or tablet. Drone cameras have become a useful tool for journalists because they're smaller and cheaper than the full-sized helicopters typically used by news outlets. Hollywood studios have even started using drones to film movies, commercials, and television shows.

SMARTPHONE

Digital cameras are standard equipment on most drones available to consumers. Many business and entertainment companies use drones because their cameras can take pictures or record video.

LIGHTS, CAMERA, ACTION!

The Federal Aviation Administration (FAA) controls and regulates civilian drone use in the United States. The FAA has rules for recreational drone flight, which include laws about not flying near people or aircraft, flying no higher than 400 feet (122 m), and keeping your drone in sight at all times. The first commercial drones allowed to fly over American soil were used to inspect oil pipelines in Alaska.

MOVIE MAGIC

In the past, many films used CGI, or computer-generated imagery, to create special effects. Footage taken by drones may be able to replace CGI, giving audiences a more realistic viewing experience.

Film sets are busy and crowded places. In the future, drones equipped with cameras could be a common sight on set, taking the place of larger, bulkier cameras.

When the FAA allowed drones to operate in the United States, the entertainment industry decided to take advantage of the new **technology**. In September 2014, the FAA allowed six movie and television production companies to begin using drones equipped with cameras on certain movie and television sets. Although drones had been used in filmmaking in other countries, this was the first time they were allowed in the United States.

Many people believe drones could **revolutionize** the film and television industries. Camera-equipped drones not only provide beautiful aerial shots, but they can also be used to get up close to the action or film in places larger helicopter-mounted cameras can't reach. In addition, drones can be used to film elaborate acrobatic shots, creating an exciting filmgoing experience. Camera drones are also cheaper, safer, and more environmentally friendly than helicopters.

The drones used for Hollywood productions need to have larger cameras than those that can be carried on a recreational drone. They also require a part called a gimbal to mount and control the camera, as well as keep it steady. To carry this additional weight, most Hollywood drones need more than the four rotors common on most consumer drones.

MORE WEIGHT, MORE ROTORS

The bigger and heavier a drone is, the more rotors it needs to get off the ground. A drone with six rotors is called a hexacopter. One with eight is called an octocopter.

Drones used by filmmaking companies need to be able to carry larger cameras than the ones carried by quadcopters. That's why most Hollywood drones will probably be hexacopters or octocopters.

DRONES AND THE NEWS

Journalists sometimes require aerial footage to accompany their reports. The news media commonly use helicopter-mounted cameras to get it, but camera-carrying drones could be an economical alternative. Sometimes people sell footage taken by drones to news outlets, but they need a special license to do so.

Journalist Tim Pool uses new technology, such as camera-equipped drones and live-streaming videos, in his reporting. In 2011, Pool used a drone called the "Occucopter" to film protests during the Occupy Wall Street movement. In March 2014, Brian Wilson recorded the first footage of a building collapse in New York City's Harlem neighborhood using a consumer drone. Drones could even be used to provide detailed video of traffic accidents and high-speed car chases.

TIM POOL

Drone cameras could change the way we experience the news—imagine being able to get up close to a traffic jam.

PLAY BALL!

Drones aren't just the future of Hollywood—they may be the future of sports, too. Drones are being used for a number of different tasks by teams, athletic departments, and sports TV networks. Many high school and college teams are using camera drones to film practices. The small, highly **maneuverable** machines can get footage from positions and angles that a handheld camera can't.

Camera-equipped drones are being used to provide aerial footage of sports, such as cross-country skiing and Formula One racing. Drones have been used in other countries to record sporting events such as cricket, soccer, and snowboarding. In June 2015, FOX Sports used drones to film the U.S. Open golf tournament. Drones are also being used to get exciting, up-close footage of extreme sports, such as surfing and skateboarding.

CHEATING BY REMOTE?

Some people in the sports industry are worried that drones could be used to cheat. A team could use a drone to secretly record the opposing team and learn all their plays before the game.

Drones can be a valuable tool for athletic coaches, letting them review how the players on their team perform.

DRONES AT THE THEME PARK

Theme park attractions frequently use the latest technology to improve visitors' entertainment experience. In the past, lasers, **holograms**, and **animatronics** have been put to use by theme parks all over the world. As drones become more popular, it should be no surprise that they could one day fly over your favorite theme parks.

A theme park in France has already started using drones to perform nightly light shows. Drones can be used as flying puppeteers, with teams of drones carrying and operating large puppets attached to strings. Drones can also be used to carry movie screens for projection shows. **Engineers** working for Disney theme parks want to use drones as "flixels," or flying **pixels**. These drones would fly over the park to create giant aerial displays that could take the place of fireworks.

INSIDE IMAGINEERING

The men and women who design and build the rides and attractions at Walt Disney theme parks are called "imagineers." Disney imagineers possess a wide range of skills, such as engineering, illustration, and graphic design.

One day, drones could take the place of fireworks and other aerial shows at theme parks around the world.

LIVE MUSIC, LIVE DRONES

For many people, concerts have become as much about the experience as they are about the music. Performers create dazzling shows involving video screens, lasers, and **pyrotechnics** to enhance the musical experience. The 2013 Vans Warped Tour was the first concert or musical festival to be recorded by a quadcopter drone. Since then, drones have become more common at large open-air concerts and other live-music events.

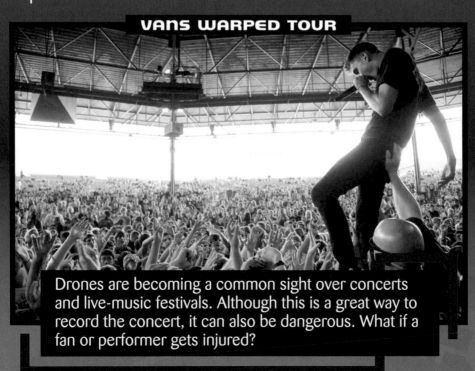

VANS WARPED TOUR

Drones are becoming a common sight over concerts and live-music festivals. Although this is a great way to record the concert, it can also be dangerous. What if a fan or performer gets injured?

CONCERT DRONE DANGER!

In June 2015, singer Enrique Iglesias was seriously injured by a drone. He raised his hand just as a drone was flying by. His hand required major surgery to fix.

Drones can provide amazing aerial footage that can either be played on video monitors around the concert or streamed directly to the Internet. Drones can also be used to get close-up footage of both the audience and the performers. Of course, there are obvious safety concerns to flying drones over several thousand people. It's the responsibility of the venue, or the place holding the concert, to make sure everyone stays safe.

ON YOUR MARK, GET SET, DRONE!

Could drone races be the future of entertainment? Some people think so. Around the world, groups of drone enthusiasts are coming together to compete in drone races.

Drone racing is a lot like racing radio-controlled cars or airplanes. The drones used for these races are small and lightweight. Many are customized, which means the operator changes them to look and perform however they want. The cameras on racing drones stream video directly to special goggles worn by their operators, letting the operators see what the drone sees as it flies. Flying a drone using first-person view, or FPV, is like playing an exciting, real-life video game. For safety reasons, these drone-racing clubs only meet and race in certain locations, such as go-cart tracks, parking lots, or warehouses, where they can be sure not to injure other people.

First-person drone racing requires the use of special goggles. The video from the drone's camera streams directly to the goggles.

THE WORLD'S SMALLEST AIR SHOW

Air shows are public events where pilots display their flying and acrobatic skills. For about a century, air shows have been popular around the world. Both civilian and military aircraft perform at these shows. Most air shows feature airplane races, military demonstrations, aerial acrobatics, and skydiving. Soon, they could also include drones.

In February 2015, a Dutch event planner announced Air 2015, the world's first drone air show. The event was advertised as a show featuring hundreds of drones flying in formation to perform ballet and circus stunts in the air. The show would feature stunt flying and drone races through a holographic 3D obstacle course. Performances would also feature music, laser effects, and video projections.

Air shows are a great place for pilots to show off their acrobatic skills. Drone pilots could one day take the place of regular pilots.

THE FAA AND DRONE SAFETY

As with any new technology, drones raise many safety concerns. Safety is one of the reasons the FAA created its guidelines for civilian drone use. Drones aren't allowed to fly above 400 feet (122 m) or faster than 100 miles (161 km) per hour. It's also illegal to use drones to get in the way of manned aircraft, such as airplanes or helicopters.

One of the biggest safety concerns regarding drones is how they affect people. Imagine drones flying above crowds of thousands of people. The rotors' spinning blades could cause serious injury if a drone were to fall or not work properly. There are also privacy concerns—people worry camera-equipped drones could be used to record or photograph people without their permission.

The rules and guidelines for drone flight established by the FAA are there to protect both the drone operator and the public.

THE FUTURE OF ENTERTAINMENT

While the entertainment industry has embraced drone use, there are still a number of legal and technical concerns that stand in the way. The FAA has strict rules about how drones can be operated over populated areas. The FAA has also limited the number of companies that are allowed to operate camera drones, but all this can change in the future.

Imagine a future where your favorite sports team uses drones to let you feel like you're right there on the field next to them during an important play. How about being able to stream live drone footage of a concert directly to your laptop or tablet? Drone technology is here to stay, and you can bet the entertainment industry is going to make the most of it.

GLOSSARY

animatronics: The technology involved with using electronics to animate puppets or other figures.

civilian: Not having to do with the military.

engineer: A person who builds and designs objects or structures to improve our world.

hologram: A 3D image that's formed by beams of light.

intelligence: Information that is of military or political value.

maneuverable: Able to change position easily.

payload: Passengers or cargo carried by an aircraft.

pixel: A tiny area of light on a screen that creates an image when combined with other pixels.

pyrotechnics: The use of fireworks to create a brilliant and dazzling display.

quadcopter: An aircraft with four rotors.

revolutionize: To bring about a radical change.

rotorcraft: An aircraft whose lift is generated by rotating blades.

sensor: A machine that measures a physical property, such as movement or heat, and records or responds to it.

technology: The way people do something using tools and the tools that they use.

vehicle: A machine that is powered to move on its own.

INDEX

WEBSITES

Due to the changing nature of Internet links, PowerKids Press has developed an online list of websites related to the subject of this book. This site is updated regularly. Please use this link to access the list: www.powerkidslinks.com/dron/ente